NEWSMAKERS

SIMONE BILES

GYMNASTICS LEGEND

BY HALEY WILLIAMS

Core Library

An Imprint of Abdo Publishing
abdobooks.com

Cover image: Simone Biles received first place on floor exercise during the 2023 US Gymnastics Championships.

abdobooks.com

Published by Abdo Publishing, a division of ABDO, PO Box 398166, Minneapolis, Minnesota 55439.

Printed in the United States of America, North Mankato, Minnesota.
102024
012025

THIS BOOK CONTAINS RECYCLED MATERIALS

Cover Photo: Laurence Griffiths/Getty Images Sport/Getty Images
Interior Photos: Ian MacNicol/Getty Images Sport/Getty Images, 4–5; Krizz DaPaul/iStockphoto, 8 (floor, beam); Shutterstock Images, 8 (vault), 40; Soeren Stache/dpa/picture alliance/Getty Images, 9; Kohjiro Kinno/Sports Illustrated Classic/Getty Images, 10–11; Smiley N. Pool/Houston Chronicle/Hearst Newspapers/Getty Images, 12; Tim Clayton/Corbis Sport/Getty Images, 16; John Thys/AFP/Getty Images, 17; Dilip Vishwanat/Getty Images Sport/Getty Images, 18–19; Alex Livesey/Getty Images Sport/Getty Images, 20; Maddie Meyer/Getty Images Sport/Getty Images, 23; Jamie Squire/Getty Images Sport/Getty Images, 24, 30; Joe Robbins/Getty Images Sport/Getty Images, 26–27; Kyodo/AP Images, 28, 43; Elsa/Getty Images Sport/Getty Images, 34–35, 45; Susan Walsh/AP Images, 37; Mehmet Murat Onel/Anadolu/Getty Images, 39

Editor: Kari Cornell
Series Designer: Marley Richmond

Library of Congress Control Number: 2024938368

Publisher's Cataloging-in-Publication Data

Names: Williams, Haley, author.
Title: Simone Biles: gymnastics legend / by Haley Williams
Other title: gymnastics legend
Description: Minneapolis, Minnesota: ABDO Publishing, 2025 | Series: Newsmakers | Includes online resources and index.
Identifiers: ISBN 9781098295721 (lib. bdg.) | ISBN 9798384916727 (ebook)
Subjects: LCSH: Biles, Simone, 1997---Juvenile literature. | Women gymnasts--Biography--Juvenile literature. | Olympic athletes--Biography--Juvenile literature. | African American women athletes--Biography--Juvenile literature.
Classification: DDC 796.44092--dc23

CONTENTS

CHAPTER ONE
All-Around Champion 4

CHAPTER TWO
Early Career 10

CHAPTER THREE
The Greatest of All Time 18

CHAPTER FOUR
Mental Health First 26

CHAPTER FIVE
The Comeback 34

Important Dates 42

Stop and Think 44

Glossary 46

Online Resources 47

Learn More 47

Index 48

About the Author 48

USA

CHAPTER ONE

ALL-AROUND CHAMPION

Simone Biles took a deep breath. She was competing at the 2016 Summer Olympics in Rio de Janeiro, Brazil. Only one event was left in the women's artistic gymnastics all around final. Biles needed to score at least a 13.834 on her floor routine to win the gold medal.

When the word *go* flashed on the screen, Biles skipped onto the floor. The crowd cheered as she got into her starting pose. Brazilian samba music began playing, and Biles

Simone Biles is one of the greatest gymnasts to ever live.

ARTISTIC GYMNASTICS

Artistic gymnastics is a sport in which athletes complete skills on different apparatuses. In women's artistic gymnastics, athletes compete on the floor, beam, uneven bars, and vault. Women started competing in Olympic artistic gymnastics in 1952.

was off. She danced to the corner of the floor and turned to do her first tumbling pass. Biles flew through the air, landing with a big smile.

Biles got ready for her second tumbling pass. The skill she performed this time was called the Biles. It was named after her because she was the first person ever to do the skill in a world competition. Biles landed the move gracefully, and the stadium filled with cheers. She continued dancing, leaping, and turning across the floor. For her third tumbling pass, Biles did a double-double. This is when a gymnast does two flips and two twists in the air. It was the hardest skill in Biles's routine. But she stuck the landing.

She had only one pass to go. Biles stepped into the corner. Then she ran into her final tumbling pass, a full twisting double back tuck. The crowd roared with excitement as Biles landed, and they continued cheering as she struck the final pose of her routine. Her performance left no doubt in anyone's mind. Simone Biles was the Olympic all-around champion.

THE BILES

Simone Biles's signature tumbling skill on floor is called the Biles. The Biles is a double back layout with a half twist at the end. Biles first debuted the skill at the World Championships in 2013. A skill is named after the first gymnast to successfully land it in an international competition. The skill is then added to the International Gymnastics Federation Code of Points and given a score based on its difficulty.

THE START OF A LEGEND

Simone Biles was born on March 14, 1997, in Columbus, Ohio. Her birth mother, Shanon, struggled with

THE BILES

Biles (Floor): Double layout with half twist

Biles (Vault): Roundoff, half turn on the table, two full twists

Biles II (Floor): Triple-double

Biles II (Vault): Roundoff, back handspring on the table, double pike

Biles (Beam): Double-double dismount

By 2024, Simone Biles had five gymnastics skills named after her. What do you notice about the skills and the apparatuses on which they were completed? Do you think adding original skills has helped Biles become successful in competitions?

addiction, and her birth father was not in her life. At the age of three, Simone and her three siblings were put into foster care. Simone was in and out of foster care for several years.

In 2003, when Simone was six, her grandfather Ron Biles and his wife, Nellie Biles, officially adopted her and

Biles's favorite event is floor.

her younger sister, Adria. Ron's sister adopted Simone's two older siblings. Simone and Adria moved to Spring, Texas, with Ron and Nellie. This is where Simone's road to becoming an Olympic champion began.

EXPLORE ONLINE

Chapter One discusses artistic gymnastics. The article at the website below goes into more depth on this topic. Does the article answer any of the questions you had about artistic gymnastics?

HOW LONG HAS GYMNASTICS BEEN A SPORT?

abdocorelibrary.com/simone-biles

NIKE

CHAPTER TWO

EARLY CAREER

At six years old, Simone went on a day care field trip to Bannon's Gymnastix in Houston, Texas. She watched as older gymnasts practiced their skills and began copying what they were doing. The coaches at the gym were impressed with Simone's skills. They sent Simone home with a letter urging her parents to sign her up for gymnastics.

Ron and Nellie had noticed that Simone had lots of energy. She would often climb

Biles considers Ron, *left*, and Nellie, *right*, to be her parents.

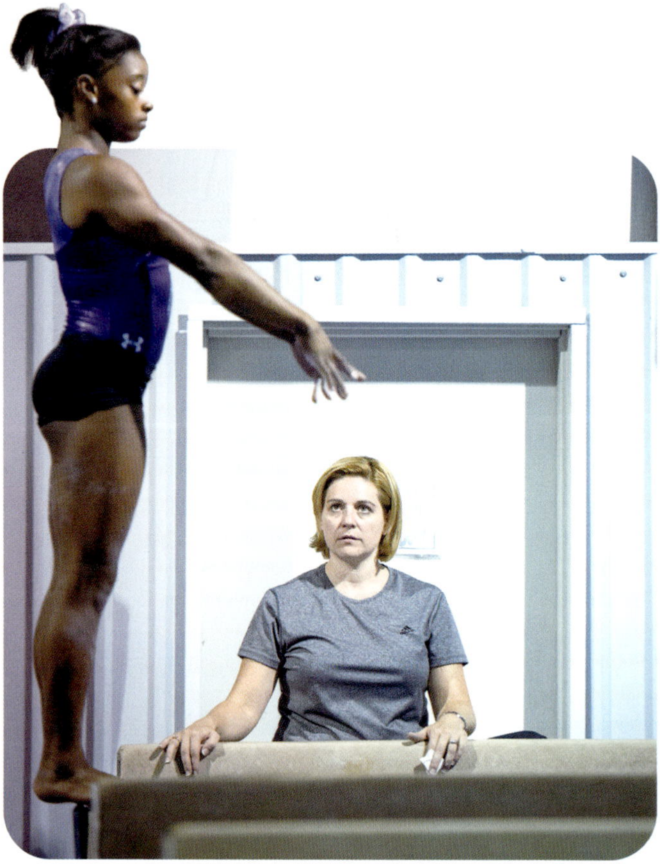

Boorman, *right*, coached Biles for 12 years.

and jump on things. They decided to sign her up for gymnastics classes at Bannon's. One of the coaches there was Aimee Boorman. Simone began training with Boorman in a Junior Olympic program when she was about seven years old.

MAKING THE NEXT MOVE

From the very beginning, Simone grabbed the attention of coaches. Her energy and strength helped her when she was training. She was able to pick up new skills quickly. This allowed Simone to move up in the competitive gymnastics levels much faster than usual.

But other parts of Simone's life were challenging. The same energy that led her to excel at gymnastics made school difficult. She had trouble focusing in class. Simone was eventually diagnosed with attention deficit hyperactivity disorder (ADHD). This is a disorder that can make it difficult for people to focus or sit still. Simone was given medication

GYMNASTICS LEVELS

Gymnasts go through ten levels before they compete in elite gymnastics. Each level has skill requirements that gymnasts must meet on each apparatus. Once gymnasts complete the required skills, they can move up to the next level. In levels one through three, gymnasts learn basic skills. They do not compete. In levels four through seven, gymnasts perform set routines to show they can do certain skills. In levels eight through ten, gymnasts learn their own routines. Once they master certain skills, they can move on to elite gymnastics.

for her ADHD. It helped her stay on task both in school and during training.

By 2011, 14-year-old Simone had begun her junior elite career. Gymnasts must be between 11 and 15 to compete at the junior elite level. That year, Simone competed at the Visa National Championships in Saint Paul, Minnesota. The top 13 athletes were selected for the Junior National Team. The team would compete in international competitions.

Simone finished fourteenth in the all-around and did not make the team. The loss made her question whether she was good enough to compete. However, Simone continued training. She also decided to do homeschooling. This allowed her to train more during the day.

That training paid off. In 2012, Simone finished first in the all-around at both the American Classic and the US Classic competitions. She also finished first on vault. At the 2012 USA Gymnastics National Championships, she finished first on vault and third in the all-around.

This was enough to earn her a spot on the Junior National Team.

OLYMPIC AGE

In 1971, gymnasts had to be at least 14 years old by the end of the year to compete in the Olympics. At that time, many people in the gymnastics community believed that the best time for gymnasts to compete was between the ages of 14 and 18. In 1981, the minimum age rose to 15. This was done in part so athletes' bodies could mature more in order to perform harder skills. In 1997, the age rose to 16. In the years since, many gymnasts have continued competing into their 20s and 30s.

THE ROAD TO RIO

At 15 years old, Simone was too young to compete at the 2012 Summer Olympics in London, England. So she focused on improving her skills. Competing in the 2016 Olympics in Rio became her goal. In 2013, Simone made her senior elite debut at 16. She competed at the American Cup, placing second in the all-around and first on vault. She was also seventh on beam and fourth on floor.

Biles won silver medals in all four events at the 2013 USA Gymnastics National Championships.

In August, Simone won the all-around at the USA Gymnastics National Championships. The win secured her a place on the Senior National Team. In late 2013, she traveled to Antwerp, Belgium, to compete in the World Gymnastics Championships. It was there that she captured the world's attention. Simone won gold in the all-around competition. She was the first Black woman to win the title. She also debuted the Biles on floor, a skill that is named after her.

In 2014 Simone won the all-around at both the US and World championships. Then in 2015, Simone

Biles won four medals at the 2013 P&G Gymnastics Championships.

became only the second woman in history to win three straight US all-around titles. At the World Championships later that year, she became the first woman to win three straight world all-around titles. Her four medals at the competition brought her total medal count to 14. Ten of those were gold. Simone had earned the most world medals of any US gymnast, and the most gold medals of any female gymnast in history.

At the end of 2015, 18-year-old Simone earned the US Olympic Committee Female Olympic Athlete of the Year. Many people saw her as the favorite going into the 2016 Olympics. And Simone did not disappoint.

2
1

CHAPTER THREE

THE GREATEST OF ALL TIME

Leading up to the 2016 Rio Olympics, Biles continued to dominate competitions. She won the all-around at the P&G Women's Gymnastics Championships. At the US Olympic Trials in early July 2016, Biles won the all-around, floor, and vault titles. It was no surprise that she earned a place on the US women's Olympic gymnastics team.

Biles's power and level of difficulty were unmatched at her first Olympic Games.

Biles won her fourth-straight US all-round title at the 2016 P&G Championships.

During the 2016 Olympic Games, Biles helped the US women's gymnastics team finish more than eight points ahead of any other country.

She helped lead Team USA to its second straight Olympic gold medal in the women's team finals. The team won by more than eight points. Biles also won gold in the all-around, floor, and vault finals. She was the fifth female gymnast in history to win four gold medals in one Olympics. She also won the bronze medal on beam, bringing her medal count to five. At the end of the Rio Games, she was given the honor of carrying the US flag at the closing ceremony. Biles had cemented her name as one of the greatest gymnasts of all time.

US OLYMPIC ALL-AROUND CHAMPIONS

The women's gymnastics individual all-around title was first awarded in 1952. Since then, six US women have won gold in the all-around. The first was Mary Lou Retton. She won the title at the 1984 Olympics in Los Angeles, California. Then from 2004 to 2024, the United States won the individual all-around title at every Olympics. Gymnasts Carly Patterson, Nastia Liukin, Gabby Douglas, Simone Biles, and Sunisa Lee were the winners, with Biles winning twice.

LIFE AFTER RIO

In September 2016, just a month after the Olympics, Biles's skills and power were called into question. Internet hackers shared some of Biles's medical records. This included information

GOLDIE THE GOAT

Many people call Biles the GOAT, an acronym standing for "greatest of all time." In 2021, Biles added sparkles in the shape of a goat to some of her leotards. She wore those leotards to several major competitions. Biles even named the goat Goldie. Her fans loved it. In an interview, Biles said the reason she put Goldie on her leotards was to stand up to her haters. She believed it was important to show kids that it's okay to feel proud of their accomplishments and talents.

about a medication she took called Ritalin. The hackers said she was using illegal substances while competing at the Olympics. Biles and USA Gymnastics quickly responded to the accusations. Biles posted on social media about using the medication to treat her ADHD. USA Gymnastics also confirmed that Biles had been given official permission to use the medication. She hadn't broken any rules. Biles used the opportunity to share the importance of breaking the stigma around ADHD.

Even after moving to Florida, Boorman, *left*, said she would always be there for Biles as a mentor.

When the Olympics ended, Biles decided to take a break from gymnastics. She wanted to have time to travel and rest. But even during her break, Biles continued to get attention for her performance in Rio.

RETURN TO TRAINING

Biles knew she wanted to compete at the 2020 Summer Olympics in Tokyo, Japan. But when her coach, Aimee Boorman, moved to Florida, Biles had to look for a new coach. The coaching team of Laurent and Cecile Landi had been successful for many years. After Biles

In 2023, Laurent Landi, *left*, and Cecile Landi, *right*, became members of the USA Gymnastics Hall of Fame for their work as coaches.

and her mom interviewed the Landis, they became her new coaches. In late 2017, Biles announced her return to training.

Many people were excited for Biles's comeback. They watched for news about when she would next compete. However, in January 2018, Biles shared news people didn't expect. She came forward as a victim of former Team USA doctor Larry Nassar. Nassar was arrested in late 2016 for assaulting many female athletes. He was found guilty and was sentenced to life in prison.

Biles and other gymnasts came forward to share their stories. Biles spoke about wanting USA Gymnastics held accountable for its role in allowing Nassar to continue his abuse for so long. She believed it was important to speak up to prevent that kind of abuse from happening again.

FURTHER EVIDENCE

Chapter Three includes information about Simone Biles becoming one of the greatest gymnasts of all time. What was one of the main points of this chapter? What evidence is included to support this point? Read the article at the website below. Does the information on the website support the main point of the chapter? Does it present new evidence?

SIMONE BILES: THE GREATEST OF ALL TIME

abdocorelibrary.com/simone-biles

CHAPTER FOUR

MENTAL HEALTH FIRST

The US Classic in July 2018 was Biles's first competition after taking a break. She picked up right where she left off. Biles won the competition by more than one point. Less than a month later, she made history at the US Gymnastics Championships. Biles placed first in the all-around and in all four events. She was the second woman ever to do so.

The 2018 World Championships in Doha, Qatar, again showed Biles's athletic greatness.

Biles competed at the 2018 GK US Classic gymnastic seniors event in Columbus, Ohio.

In 2018, Biles became the first woman to win four all-around titles at the World Championships.

She won gold in the team, all-around, floor, and vault finals. She also won a silver on the uneven bars and a bronze on the beam. No other American woman had won a medal in each event at the world championships before. In addition, Biles had a new skill named after her on vault.

At the 2019 World Championships in Stuttgart, Germany, Biles won her twenty-fifth world medal. She was officially the most decorated gymnast ever. She also had two new skills named after her at the competition.

One was on floor and the other was on beam.

Biles seemed to be on her way to major success at the 2020 Olympics.

THE ROAD TO TOKYO

The COVID-19 pandemic put a stop to gymnastics competitions in 2020. The International Olympic Committee decided to delay the Olympics. The Games were rescheduled for the summer of 2021.

The break in competing didn't seem to affect Biles. At the 2021 US Classic, Biles performed one of the most difficult vaults in the world. It is called a Yurchenko double pike. No woman had ever landed the vault in competition before. But Biles made it look easy.

Biles continued her dominance leading up to the Tokyo Olympics in 2021. She won her seventh US all-around title at the 2021 US Championships. She medaled in all four events at the competition. Biles also won the all-around at the US Olympic Trials. Once again, Biles made the women's Olympic team.

During the 2021 US Championships, Biles won gold for all-around, beam, floor, and vault.

THE TOKYO OLYMPICS

Many people expected Biles to win five medals at the Tokyo Olympics in 2021. She was also expected to be the first woman in about 50 years to win back-to-back all-around titles. But Team USA had a shaky start at the Games. On qualification night, Biles and several of her teammates made mistakes. During her floor routine, Biles bounced out of bounds and almost fell. She also stepped out of bounds on her vault and took several steps on her beam dismount. The mistakes landed the team in second place going into the finals.

But Biles still qualified for the individual all-around competition.

A day after the team qualifications, Biles posted on social media about the pressures of competing. Two days later, Biles barely landed her jump on vault during the team final. Then she shocked the world when she withdrew from the team finals and the individual all-around. Biles said she was suffering from the twisties. This is a mental block that causes gymnasts to lose their awareness in the air while twisting. Both Biles and her coaches were worried she would injure herself if she continued to compete.

COVID-19 AND THE OLYMPICS

On July 8, 2021, the Japanese Olympic Committee announced that no fans would be allowed at the Tokyo Olympics. This decision was made to prevent the spread of the COVID-19 virus. Without crowds at the events, stadiums and fields were much quieter than normal. Some athletes said they were able to prepare themselves for the quiet. But other athletes, including Biles, later talked about how the lack of a crowd affected their performance.

Biles received a lot of criticism for withdrawing. Critics said if Biles had competed, the team would have won gold instead of silver. But Biles didn't back down. She became an advocate for prioritizing mental health. Biles said it was important for athletes to put their mental health first in order to continue succeeding in and enjoying their sport.

Although Biles didn't defend her all-around title, she did come back to compete in the beam final. She won a bronze medal, bringing her total Olympic medal count to seven.

SUNISA LEE

Sunisa Lee is an American gymnast from Saint Paul, Minnesota. She was a member of the US Olympic team at the Tokyo Olympics in 2021. Lee qualified for the individual all-around competition along with Simone Biles. When Biles dropped out, Lee went on to win gold in the all-around competition. She became the first Asian American woman to win the title. Lee also competed at the 2024 Paris Olympics, winning bronze medals in the individual all-around and in the uneven bars final.

STRAIGHT TO THE SOURCE

Many professional athletes supported Biles's decision to withdraw from some of the competitions in Tokyo. Olympic gold-medal swimmer Michael Phelps was one of her biggest supporters. He discussed how Biles's withdrawal shows the importance of providing mental health support for athletes:

> *I hope this is an opportunity for us to jump on board and to even blow this mental health thing even more wide open. . . . We carry a lot of weight on our shoulders and it's challenging, especially when we have the lights on us and all of these expectations being thrown on top of us.*

Source: "Michael Phelps on Simone Biles, Mental Health: 'It's OK to Not Be OK.'" *Athletic*, 27 July 2021, theathletic.com. Accessed 1 Apr. 2024.

BACK IT UP

The author of this passage is using evidence to support a point. Write a paragraph describing the point the author is making. Then write down two or three pieces of evidence the author uses to make the point.

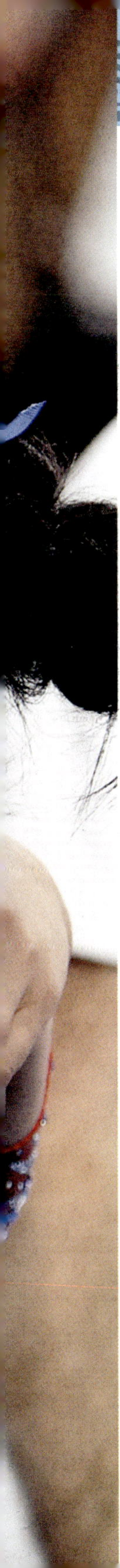

CHAPTER FIVE

THE COMEBACK

Biles knew she needed to step away from gymnastics after the Tokyo Olympics. It was time to put her mental health first. In an interview, Biles shared that she felt like a failure after the Olympics. But she also knew her decision to withdraw was the right one. Biles was open about going to therapy to help her with her mental health struggles.

Some of these challenges stemmed from the abuse she'd suffered. In September 2021,

After Biles stepped away from gymnastics, her teammates rallied to support her.

Biles spoke at a trial against Larry Nassar. She and several other gymnasts shared their stories.

Despite the challenges Biles faced, she continued to move forward. In February 2022, she announced her engagement to professional football player Jonathan Owens. The couple got married the next year. President Joe Biden honored Biles with the Presidential Medal of Freedom in 2022. The Presidential Medal of Freedom is given to people who have made significant contributions to the United States. Biles was awarded for her athletic accomplishments as well as her advocacy for mental health, foster children, and survivors of

FEMALE ATHLETE OF THE YEAR

In December 2023, the Associated Press (AP) named Biles AP Female Athlete of the Year. She received the award after her successful comeback in 2023. Biles was the sixth female athlete to win the award three times. She had also won in 2016 and 2019.

Biles considers the Presidential Medal of Freedom to be the greatest award she's received.

sexual abuse. She became the youngest person in history to receive the award.

THE ROAD TO PARIS

In June 2023, Biles announced her comeback to gymnastics. She said she had prioritized her mental and physical health during her break. She had a new mindset as she prepared to go into training. Biles set her sights on competing in the 2024 Olympics in Paris, France.

Biles's first competition after her break was in August 2023. She shared her nerves with fans online,

MAKING HISTORY

The 2023 World Championships was a historic event for women of color. Simone Biles won gold, Rebeca Andrade of Brazil won silver, and American Shilese Jones won bronze. It was the first time that three women of color were on the all-around awards podium at a World Championships.

but those nerves didn't seem to affect her performance. Biles won first in the all-around by five points. Later that month, Biles wowed the world again by winning her eighth US all-around title at the US Championships. At 26, she was the oldest woman to win the title.

Her success didn't stop there. Her first international competition since the Tokyo Olympics was the 2023 World Championships in Antwerp, Belgium. Biles came away with her sixth all-around gold medal. She won gold in the team, floor, and beam finals as well. And she won silver on vault, despite falling on the landing. Biles also had a fifth skill named after her on the apparatus.

Biles became the oldest US gymnast to win gold at the 2024 Olympics.

But Biles wasn't done yet. At the 2024 Olympics, she finished her comeback with a bang. Despite competing against the talented Rebeca Andrade of Brazil, Biles secured the all-around gold for the second time. She also helped the United States win gold in

SIMONE BILES'S MEDALS

30 gold (7 Olympic, 23 World Championship)	6 silver (2 Olympic, 4 World Championship)	5 bronze (2 Olympic, 3 World Championship)

By the end of the 2024 Paris Olympics, Simone Biles had won 41 medals in major international competitions. With 30 gold medals, she is the most successful gymnast in World Championships history. Do you think Biles's success could help grow the sport of gymnastics around the world? Why or why not?

the team final. With another gold on vault and a silver on floor, Biles brought her Olympic medal count to 11. She also broke the record for most gold medals won by a US gymnast. She had 41 international medals in all, which was the most of any gymnast in history.

Simone Biles is a legend in the sport of gymnastics. Since her elite debut in 2011, she has gained attention worldwide for her talent, hard work, and advocacy. Biles will go down as one of the greatest gymnasts in history.

STRAIGHT TO THE SOURCE

After Biles announced her comeback, many people wondered how she would handle the pressure of competing again. In a September 2023 interview, Biles discussed how her approach during her comeback had been different in a positive way:

> *I think what success means to me is a little bit different than before because before, everyone defined success for me, even if I had my own narrative that I wanted. . . . So now, it's just showing up, being in a good head place, having fun out there, and whatever happens, happens.*

Source: Scott Bregman. "Exclusive—Simone Biles on Letting Go, Twisting Again, and Having No Regrets: 'What Success Means to Me Is Different Than Before.'" *Olympics*, 27 Sept. 2023, olympics.com. Accessed 1 Apr. 2024.

WHAT'S THE BIG IDEA?

Take a close look at this passage. What is the main connection between Biles's comeback and her focus on mental health? How do you think having a different approach to competing has helped Biles make her comeback? Include two supporting details.

IMPORTANT DATES

March 14, 1997
Simone Biles is born in Columbus, Ohio.

2003
Ron and Nellie Biles officially adopt Simone and her younger sister. Simone begins taking gymnastics classes.

2013
At the World Championships, Simone becomes the first Black woman to win gold in the all-around competition. She also gets her first skill named after her.

2015
Biles becomes the first woman to win three straight World Championships and the second to win three straight US Championships.

2016
At the Rio Olympics, Biles wins four gold medals, including one in the all-around individual competition. She also wins bronze on beam.

2018
Biles medals in all four events and in the all-around at the World Championships in Doha, Qatar. She is the first US woman to do so.

2021
Biles withdraws from the all-around and team finals at the Tokyo Olympics. She becomes an advocate for prioritizing mental health.

2024
Biles wins gold in the all-around, team, and vault finals and silver on floor at the 2024 Paris Olympics.

STOP AND THINK

Surprise Me

Chapter Two discusses Simone Biles's early gymnastics career. After reading this book, what two or three facts about her career did you find most surprising? Write a few sentences about each fact. Why did you find each fact surprising?

Dig Deeper

After reading this book, what questions do you still have about Simone Biles? With an adult's help, find a few reliable sources that can help you answer your questions. Write a paragraph about what you learned.

Say What?

Studying important figures can mean learning a lot of new vocabulary. Find five words in this book you've never heard before. Use a dictionary to find out what they mean. Then write the meanings in your own words and use each word in a new sentence.

Another View

This book talks about Simone Biles withdrawing from the Tokyo Olympics in 2021. As you know, every source is different. Ask a librarian or another adult to help you find a second source about this event. Write a short essay comparing and contrasting the new source's point of view with that of this book's author. What is the point of view of each author? How are they similar and why? How are they different and why?

GLOSSARY

advocate
a person who stands up for a cause or an idea

assaulting
inappropriately touching or violently handling another person

debut
to make a first appearance

dismount
in gymnastics, a skill or move done to get off an apparatus at the end of a routine

foster care
a government system in which children are placed with new caregivers for a time when their guardians are unable to care for them

hacker
a person who illegally accesses information through a computer

pandemic
a disease outbreak that happens across multiple countries or around the world

qualify
to complete certain requirements or conditions for something

stigma
beliefs of a society or group that are negative or unfair about something

ONLINE RESOURCES

To learn more about Simone Biles, visit our free resource websites below.

Core Library CONNECTION
FREE! COMMON CORE MULTIMEDIA RESOURCES

Visit **abdocorelibrary.com** or scan this QR code for free Common Core resources for teachers and students, including vetted activities, multimedia, and booklinks, for deeper subject comprehension.

Booklinks NONFICTION NETWORK
FREE! ONLINE NONFICTION RESOURCES

Visit **abdobooklinks.com** or scan this QR code for free additional online weblinks for further learning. These links are routinely monitored and updated to provide the most current information available.

LEARN MORE

Loh, Stefanie. *Who Is Simone Biles?* Penguin Workshop, 2023.

Monnig, Alex. *Gymnastics*. Abdo, 2023.

Wetzel, Dan. *Epic Athletes: Simone Biles*. Henry Holt, 2020.

INDEX

attention deficit hyperactivity disorder (ADHD), 13–14, 22

Bannon's Gymnastix, 11–12
Biles, Nellie, 8–9, 11–12, 24
Biles, Ron, 8–9, 11–12
Biles, the, 6–8, 16, 28–29, 38
Boorman, Aimee, 12, 23

Junior National Team, 14–15
Junior Olympic program, 12

Landi, Cecile, 23–24
Landi, Laurent, 23–24
Lee, Sunisa, 21, 32
London Olympics, 15

mental health, 31–33, 35–37, 41

Nassar, Larry, 25, 36

Paris Olympics, 32, 37, 39, 40
Presidential Medal of Freedom, 36

Rio Olympics, 5, 15, 19, 21, 23

Team USA, 20, 25, 30–32
Tokyo Olympics, 23, 29–33, 35, 38
twisties, the, 31

US Classic competitions, 14, 27, 29
US Olympic Committee Female Olympic Athlete of the Year, 17
US Olympic Trials, 19, 29
USA Gymnastics National Championships, 14, 16

About the Author

Haley Williams is an editor who lives in Minnesota. In her free time, she enjoys reading, coaching softball, and watching movies. Her favorite sport to watch during the Olympics is gymnastics.